# ARNOLD SCHWARZENEGGER

# Man of Action
## by Daniel Bial

A Book Report Biography
FRANKLIN WATTS
A Division of Grolier Publishing
New York / London / Hong Kong / Sydney
Danbury, Connecticut

Y
791.43
BIA
I

frontispiece: *Arnold Schwarzenegger as Conan the Barbarian*
Cover illustration by Doug Rugh,
interpreted from a photograph by Gamma Liason

Photographs ©: AP/Wide World Photos: 30, 46, 48, 65, 76;
Archive Photos: 36, 78, 44 (Darlene Hammond); Globe Photos: 49
(Michael Norcia) 97 (Alpha/Steve Finn) 2, 21, 69, 85, 96, 98; International
Federation of Bodybuilders, Montreal, Canada: 42; Gammma Liason: 92
(Allen), 94; MuscleMag: 50; Museum of Modern Art: 61, 87, 90; Photofest:
32, 80; President's Council on Physical Fitness and Sports: 83; Retna
Ltd/Camera Press Ltd.: 18, Shooting Star Photography: 100 (Theo
Kingma), 11, 16, 20, 26, 27, 58 (Michael Montfort), 55 (S. Murphy), 38;
UPI/Corbis/Bettmann: 22, 67, 74; Weider Photo Library: 34, 40.

Visit Franklin Watts on the Internet at:
http://publishing.grolier.com

Library of Congress Cataloging-in-Publication Data

Bial, Daniel, 1955–
    Arnold Schwarzenegger : man of action / Daniel Bial.
        p. cm.—(A book report biography)
    Includes bibliographical references and index.
    Summary: A biography of the Austrian-born bodybuilder who has
become a Hollywood star.
    ISBN 0-531-11485-6 (lib.bdg.) ISBN 0-531-15933-7 (pbk)
    1. Schwarzenegger, Arnold—Juvenile literature. 2. Motion picture
actors and actresses—United States—Biography—Juvenile literature.
3. Bodybuilders—United States—Biography—Juvenile literature.
[1. Schwarzenegger, Arnold. 2. Actors and actresses. 3. Bodybuilders.]
I. Title. II. Series.
PN2287.S3368B53 1998
791.43'028'092—dc21
[b]                                                                          97-29323
                                                                                CIP
                                                                                 AC

# CONTENTS

# ARNOLD SCHWARZENEGGER

# CHAPTER ONE

# MR. UNIVERSE

The crowd at the Royal Hotel in London knew they were witnessing something historic. They stood and cheered, hanging on every move of the young man on stage. Clad in only brief swim trunks, the man stood facing the audience, holding his arms up, flexing his biceps. He held the pose for a few seconds, then looked to his left, showing his amazing neck muscles.

Arnold Schwarzenegger, at age twenty, was a truly outstanding physical specimen. Standing 6'2" (188 cm) and weighing 250 pounds (113 kg), he didn't have an ounce of fat on him. He was all pure, rippling muscle. His biceps were 21 inches (53 cm) around. His torso was shaped like a V: his chest measured 57 inches (145 cm) around and yet his waist was only 33 inches (84 cm). His 28-inch (71-cm) thighs were nearly as big as his waist, and his calves were 18 inches (46 cm). He was as strong as he looked, capable of bench-pressing 500 pounds (227 kg). Although he had the body of a Greek god, Schwarzenegger's face was still boyish. He wore his hair short, and his eyes gleamed with enthusiasm.

The year was 1967. Arnold had already won several important bodybuilding titles, but this was the world's most important bodybuilding competition—the Mr. Universe contest. The best bodybuilders in the world were competing, and no one as young as Arnold had ever won.

The previous year, Arnold had won three important contests: Best Built Man of Europe, Mr. Europe, and the International Powerlifting Championship. Still, he was little known when he arrived for his first Mr. Universe contest that year. Defending champion Chet Yorton won his second title in a row, while Arnold finished second. Many onlookers felt that he should have won that contest—Arnold was the audience favorite—but the judges felt his legs needed work. Arnold took the criticism to heart. The next time he went to the gym, he had cut his trousers off at the knee. He wanted everyone there to make fun of his legs so that he would work harder on that part of his body.

At the 1967 Mr. Universe contest, no one criticized his legs. But it wasn't only Arnold's body

*Arnold Schwarzenegger strikes a pose in the summer of 1966, the year before he won his first Mr. Universe title.*

that had the crowd going crazy. It was also the way he posed. He had more grace than the others, moving from one pose to the next with almost balletic ease.

He also knew how to play to the audience. Arnold chose to perform his routine accompanied by the inspiring music from the film *Exodus*. There was an arrogance, a swagger in his posing. The half smile on his face seemed both to beg for the audience's approval and yet to say that he didn't need it.

Bodybuilding judges look for many things as they tally their scores. They look for immense muscles, of course, but they also look for body symmetry—in bodybuilding the development of all the body's muscles should be harmonious. They also award points for presentation and style. And they aren't fooled when a contestant tries to hide a weak spot in his or her build.

"Posing is pure theatre," Arnold later wrote in his book, *Arnold: Education of a Bodybuilder* (1985). "I understand that and I love it. There are bodybuilders who put almost no time into posing. And, of course, they don't win." In 1967, Arnold broke through and won the title that would launch his international career.

**"Posing is pure theatre."**

"He's got the biggest dose of charisma I've ever seen in a bodybuilder," wrote Ivan Dunbar in *Health and Strength* magazine.

# A MAN WITH A PLAN

After the contest, Arnold stayed at the home of a new friend, Wag Bennett; Bennett's wife, Diane; and their six children. Although Arnold spoke little English, he was fully prepared when Wag, a judge at the Mr. Universe contest, asked him what his life's ambitions were.

"Most bodybuilders would say, 'I want to be Mr. Britain, Mr. Universe, etc.,'" Wag said. "Then I would say, 'Yeah?' But that was it. That was the height of their ambition."

Arnold, on the other hand, had made big plans for the rest of his life:

> I will come to America, which is the country for me. Once [t]here, I will become the greatest bodybuilder in history.... I will go to college so I can get a business degree. Simultaneously, I will make whatever money possible from bodybuilding and invest it in real estate. I will go into movies as an actor, producer and eventually director. By the time I am thirty, I will have starred in my first movie and I will be a millionaire. I will collect houses, art and automobiles. I will see the world. Along the way I will learn to impress

people and I will hone my mind to outwit all of them.

I will marry a glamorous and intelligent wife. By thirty-two I will have been invited to the White House.

Arnold had devotion, drive, and the daring to dream big. Bennett may have shaken his head in amazement at hearing Arnold's plans. But every one of them would come true—and then some.

# CHAPTER TWO

# EARLY YEARS

In 1938, Germany annexed, or incorporated into its own territory, the neighboring country of Austria just before World War II. At the time, Germany was led by the Austrian-born Adolf Hitler, and many Austrians felt a kinship with the goals of Hitler's Third Reich, which aimed to expand Germany's powers. That same year, Gustav Schwarzenegger signed up with Hitler's Nazi party, as soon as it was legal for Austrians to do so.

After Germany's defeat in World War II, Austria regained its independence. Gustav became the police chief and leader of the local police marching band in Thal, Austria, a town of about 1,200 people in the beautiful Tyrol mountains. He married Aurelia right after the war ended in 1945, and they quickly had two children: Meinhard, who was born in 1946, and Arnold, who came a year later, on July 30, 1947.

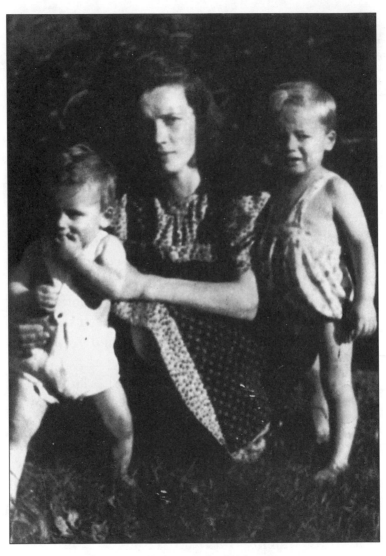

*Arnold (left) poses with his mother and
older brother, Meinhard.*

Gustav was a tough father. He held contests to see which of his sons was better at running, boxing, skiing, and doing their homework. The older and stronger Meinhard usually won, and Gustav would further humiliate Arnold by making him admit that he was inferior. Sometimes when Arnold won, Gustav would repeat the contest to give Meinhard an extra chance.

The Schwarzeneggers often went on outings to concerts and museums to enrich the boys' cultural knowledge. Meinhard and Arnold liked the trips—but they knew that when they returned home Gustav would make them write long essays on what they had seen and done. Gustav was a stickler for accuracy, good grammar, and correct spelling.

Money was tight in the Schwarzenegger house. They had no indoor plumbing, and Aurelia, a mild-mannered woman, had to haul heavy buckets of water up and down the stairs. Gustav had a violent temper and sometimes drank too much. Then he would tear up the house, screaming and striking at whoever got in his way.

Arnold was not a happy child. His father scared him and told him that he was worthless. Even at the age of thirteen, Arnold sometimes wet his pants. Often Arnold took his unhappiness out on other children. He and Meinhard were bullies who beat up their classmates and threw their

*Johnny Weissmuller was a strong man famous*
*for his role as Tarzan.*

books in the lake. There's even a story that the two brothers beat up a milkman. When he complained to their father, Police Chief Gustav convinced the man to forget about it.

While Meinhard thrived on being his parents' clear favorite, Arnold struggled to find his place in the world. About the only thing he was sure of was that he liked power. "Ever since I was a child, I would say to myself, 'There must **"I wanted to be different."** be more to life than this,'" he said in an interview. "I wanted to be different. I wanted to be part of the small percentage of people who were leaders, not the large mass of followers."

## FINDING HIS PLACE

One of the few things Arnold truly loved were movies, especially films about powerful people. He went to the nearby city of Graz to watch films starring strong men. He loved John Wayne and Johnny Weissmuller (who made many Tarzan flicks). Arnold was particularly fond of Steve Reeves and Reg Park, who starred in movies about the ancient Greek hero Hercules. Both Reeves and Park were bodybuilders, each a former Mr. Universe. They strolled around the movies wearing togas that showed off their large

*Arnold works on a drawing in art class in 1958.*

builds. Most people preferred Reeves in these roles, but Arnold was partial to Park. When Park picked up a boulder and threw it as if it weighed nothing or tossed villains around as if they posed no threat to him, Arnold was extremely impressed.

Very near to the movie theater in Graz was a bodybuilding gym run by a former Mr. Austria, Kurt Marnul. Marnul invited both Schwarzenegger boys to train with him. At first, Marnul thought Meinhard had the greater future in bodybuilding because he had slender hips, broad shoulders, and an easy-going personality that seemed perfect for the sport. But Meinhard never cared much for the discipline and soon gave it up. Arnold, on the other hand, loved bodybuilding and started to dedicate himself to it entirely. Arnold was fourteen years old when he started bodybuilding. He was 6'2" (188 cm) tall already, but very thin, weighing only 150 pounds (68 kg).

Arnold was good at sports and excelled in soccer. But in bodybuilding, Arnold seemed to know immediately that he had discovered his life's call-

*Arnold (sitting second from the left)*
*and his classmates*

*Steve Reeves, pictured here in 1943, was one of Arnold's movie and bodybuilding idols.*

ing. Shortly after his first workout, Arnold turned to a boy practicing next to him and said, "Well, I give myself about five years and I will be Mr. Universe." After that session, he was so sore he had to push his bicycle back the 8 miles (13 km) to his house. The next morning, he couldn't even comb his hair due to muscle fatigue.

**"Well, I give myself about five years and I will be Mr. Universe."**

The gym was closed on Sundays, but Arnold was so dedicated he once broke a window in order to get inside for some more training. He often did reps (repetitions of lifts) after school, went home for dinner, and then returned to the gym after Gustav fell asleep. He stopped going to church and didn't pay much attention to his homework. At his first bodybuilding contest, held in a Graz hotel, he came in second, which only increased his desire to train harder.

Soon, Arnold moved to Graz to be nearer the gym. He worked as a carpenter and borrowed money from friends in order to pay for food and training. One of his new friends was Alfred Gerstl, a bodybuilding promoter. Gerstl often invited Arnold over to his house, giving him advice and feeding him the red meat that the young bodybuilder could otherwise not have afforded.

Bodybuilders need to follow a high-protein, low-fat diet. In those days, however, the dangers of cholesterol were not widely known. Arnold could easily eat a steak and eight eggs for breakfast, and some lifters ate as many as thirty eggs a day. Nowadays, lifters know there are better ways to get protein.

Arnold watched himself carefully in the mirror as he grew bigger and stronger. Under Marnul's tutelage, Arnold put on 45 pounds (20 kg) of muscle. Once, a young man impressed by Arnold's results started to follow him around, watching his workouts and pestering him with all sorts of questions. Arnold still could be a bully, but now he was more subtle about it. He told the teenager he should go on a salt diet.

The kid left the gym vowing to take Arnold's advice. As soon as the boy had left, the other bodybuilders burst out laughing. Salt is the last thing a bodybuilder wants to eat a lot of—the body retains water, and the bloating that results obscures the effect of rippling muscles. Nevertheless, the young bodybuilder ground up nutshells and ate them with one teaspoon of salt the first day, two the second day, etc. Unfortunately, the teenager did not realize he had been tricked until seventeen days later when he became quite sick.

Arnold's dedication to bodybuilding meant that he had time for few friends, but the "salt diet" caper increased his popularity in the gym. Body-builders love to psych one another out—whether by playing practical jokes or simply lifting more weights than the next person. Arnold thrived on the new attention and later repeated the diet prank with other naive kids—although he substi-tuted ice cream or sugar for salt so as not to threaten the health of his victims.

## FIRST COMPETITIONS

When Arnold was seventeen, he entered his first regional bodybuilding contest and came in second. The exposure was terrific for Arnold's career, and he set his sights on competing in the Junior Mr. Europe contest—the biggest event of the year for young bodybuilders.

By that time, however, Arnold was serving in the army. Austria drafted all fit men for a year of service when they turned eighteen. Arnold had always wanted to drive a tank, and Gustav used his influence to have Arnold stationed in a tank division near Graz. Arnold enjoyed being in the army—especially having all the food he could eat. But how could he get to Stuttgart, Germany, where the contest was being held? His superior officers would not release him from duty for the weekend.

Arnold debated what to do. He decided to take the biggest risk of his life and left the base

*Arnold enjoyed his time in the army.*
*He served in the Austrian Army's tank division.*

without permission. He scraped up enough
money to buy a third-class train ticket, but when
he arrived he needed to borrow body oil and
trunks to pose in. He knew little about how to
pose, and his body still lacked definition. Still, the
judges saw a star in the making and awarded him
first prize.

*Arnold receives congratulations after winning the
1965 Junior Mr. Europe title.*

When Arnold returned to camp, he was locked up in the stockade for a week. But at Stuttgart, he had made important friends. One was Rolf Putziger, a magazine publisher who invited Arnold to train at his gym in Munich. Another was Franco Colombu, a bodybuilder from the Italian island of Sardinia, who was also on his way to stardom.

When Arnold finished his year of army service, his parents told him it was time to settle down. They wanted him to give up bodybuilding and suggested that he either apply for a job in the local pencil factory or reenlist in the army. Arnold agreed that it was time for a change. He was only nineteen years old and had his whole life ahead of him. He packed his few belongings and moved to Munich to train full time.

# CHAPTER THREE

IN TRAINING

In Munich, Arnold set to work. He hooked up with his friend Franco Colombu, and the two spent long hours in the gym. Arnold became locally famous for how long he could work out. Other serious lifters might practice for two or three hours a day, but it was nothing for Arnold to pump iron for six or seven hours. Other bodybuilders prudently stopped when their muscles started to ache. But Arnold had a high tolerance for pain. He would push himself even to the point of throwing up or keeling over. "I have no fear of fainting," Arnold said. "I do squats until I fall over and pass out. So what? It's not going to kill me. I wake up five minutes later and I'm okay."

In a typical morning routine, Arnold would load the barbell with 500 pounds (230 kg), hoist it on his shoulders, and do a set of twelve squats, and then do ten more sets, along with other exer-

*Franco Colombu was Arnold's
training partner in Munich.*

cises as well. Arnold worked so hard because he loved what he was doing. Weightlifters get a kind of high from all the intense repetitions. Blood rushes into the active muscles to feed them and keep them going under all the stress. Arnold felt a kind of ecstasy because he could actually feel his muscles getting bigger. "Blood is rushing into your muscles, that's what we call the pump," Arnold said. "Your muscles get a really tight feeling, like you're going to explode."

**"Your muscles get a really tight feeling, like you're going to explode."**

Franco and Arnold developed a routine. One day they would work on their arm muscles (biceps and triceps), another day on the chest (pecs) and back, another on calves and thighs. Arnold would push himself as much as anyone else in Putziger's gym. And after he was finally finished with his workout, he would push a broom through the place, cleaning up in order to pay for his training fees. He also did some modeling to help pay for the huge amounts of food he ate.

## STEROIDS

Arnold has admitted that he also took steroids while training. At the time, they weren't illegal

*Arnold explains his workout techniques
at a California gym.*

and few people knew how dangerous they could be. Derived from the male hormone testosterone, steroids help build muscle tissue. But they have many side effects, including aggression, depression, acne, hair loss, and liver problems. Before football star Lyle Alzado died of brain cancer, he blamed his disease on the steroids he took.

No doubt, steroids helped Arnold reach his amazing size and bulk. He too suffered from their side effects. Steroids made him irritable and aggressive. On several occasions, Arnold ran amok, and the police had to be called in to help restore calm. But steroids aren't the reason why Arnold became a champion bodybuilder. He earned his titles through extreme hard work and dedication.

## AROUND THE WORLD

After Arnold made his first appearance at the Mr. Universe contest in London, he met his hero, Reg Park, the former Mr. Universe who starred in the Hercules movies that Arnold had watched as a child. Park was amazed when he saw the young Austrian lifter and said, "One day you are going to be the best bodybuilder in the world." Arnold was bowled over to hear such praise from the man he idolized.

Park also said, "Win the Mr. Universe title,

*South African bodybuilder and action hero
Reg Park was one of Arnold's idols and helped
the young bodybuilder start his career.*

and I'll bring you out to South Africa," where he lived. A year later, Arnold had the trophy in hand, and he telegraphed Park with the news. Park, a successful businessman, was true to his word. His luxurious house with its huge pool, expensive antiques, and many servants astonished Arnold. He was also impressed when Park offered him a contract to tour the country, posing in ten shows for 50 pounds (about 80 U.S. dollars) per appearance. Arnold needed the money.

After a brief stop back in Austria—where he got a cool reception from his old friends, who partly envied his success and partly resented his smug demeanor—Arnold had a new country to conquer: the United States. Joe Weider, the most important man in U.S. bodybuilding, saw photos of Arnold in *Iron Man* magazine and asked him to compete in the Mr. Olympia contest. Arnold flew to Miami at the end of September 1968, traveling with almost no money and just one gym bag.

Arnold again stunned the audience with his size and posing, but he was stunned himself when he finished in second place. Frank Zane, the winner, weighed 70 pounds (32 kg) less than Arnold, but his muscles were far more defined. They "seemed to have been tooled down with chisels and gouges a sculptor would use on mahogany," Arnold admitted. The night after his loss, Arnold cried himself to sleep.

*Arnold poses at the 1968 Mr. Universe competition.*

Weider, founder of the International Federation of Bodybuilders (IFBB) and owner of many bodybuilding businesses, had already made good money from Schwarzenegger. He had used a picture of Arnold on the cover of his *Muscle Power* (later *Muscle & Fitness*) magazine, and it became one of the best-selling issues. After the Mr. Olympia contest, Weider had Arnold come out to California. He paid Arnold $200 a week to train and write articles (with a lot of editorial help at first) for his magazines.

Weider also loaned him a car, although Arnold didn't know how to drive. Arnold was taking a practice spin when he got into an accident. The gear lever pierced his leg, and he had to have the wound stitched up. In typical Arnold fashion, though, he did leg exercises in that evening's workout.

Arnold returned to London to capture the Mr. Universe title in both 1968 and 1969, but he still hadn't won a U.S. competition. In 1969, Sergio Oliva, a Cuban, won the Mr. Olympia contest. The beautifully sculpted Oliva triumphed by the closest of margins—the judges split four-to-three in favor of him. It would be the last time Arnold would come in second.

## ACTING DEBUT

Weider helped Arnold fulfill one of his lifelong dreams when he recommended him to producers

*Arnold drives a chariot through Times Square in his first movie,* Hercules in New York. *For this film, he used the stage name Arnold Strong.*

who were looking for a muscleman to star in a movie. Weider told them Arnold had performed Shakespeare in Europe. In truth, Arnold had never taken an acting lesson in his life.

The movie he starred in, however, required no acting ability. If the neighborhood video store has a copy of *Hercules in New York* (also released under the name *Hercules Goes Bananas*), it's only because Arnold appears in it. The whole film cost a mere $300,000, and clearly there was no money to spend on such fineries as extra takes or a semi-intelligent script. Arnold got to run around in a toga or with his shirt off for much of the picture; he also drove a chariot through Times Square and Central Park. The one thing he didn't get a chance to do was hear his own voice. His accent was so strong that the producers had his lines dubbed. He also didn't get to see his name in lights. Weider convinced him that "Schwarzenegger" was too much of a tongue twister for American audiences. His name appears in the credits as "Arnold Strong."

## CONQUERING AMERICA

After finishing the movie, Arnold persuaded Weider to bring Franco Colombu to the United States. Colombu moved into Schwarzenegger's apartment in Santa Monica, and the two trained, learned English, and enjoyed the California singles scene together. Critics have asserted Arnold didn't want American friends because they were his competitors. Colombu, who stood only 5'5" (165 cm), won the Mr. Olympia contest twice—in 1976 and 1981—but in a different weight division from Arnold.

In 1970, Arnold won his fourth Mr. Universe

*Cuban bodybuilder Sergio Oliva edged
Schwarzenegger in the 1969 Mr. Olympia
competition, but Arnold beat him the following year.*

title, this time defeating Reg Park, who had briefly come out of retirement. The next day, Arnold made his debut on U.S. television, winning the Pro Mr. World contest in Columbus, Ohio. In beating Sergio Oliva, he won $500 and a watch.

That year, he also broke through at the Mr. Olympia contest. A year earlier, Arnold felt Oliva had psyched him out in order to win. This time, Arnold turned the tables. The finals featured Arnold versus Oliva. After a few minutes of side-by-side posing, Arnold told Oliva he was done, and the two agreed to exit the stage. Oliva walked off, but Arnold stopped, turned to the audience, and struck his most dazzling pose. The judges thought Oliva had quit, and Arnold got the victory. In doing so, he wrapped up the equivalent of body-building's triple crown: Mr. Universe, Pro Mr. World, and Mr. Olympia all in one year.

Two years later, Arnold again outsmarted Oliva. He arranged for the preliminaries to be held in a room painted in a dark color. The contrast made his body stand out more than Oliva's, whose skin was much darker than Arnold's.

## JUGGLING CAREERS

In 1971, Joe Weider forbade Arnold from defending his Mr. Universe title. Weider was in a business battle with the organization that held the

*Joe Weider, the founder of the International Federation of Bodybuilders, was an important influence on Arnold's career.*

contest and didn't want his biggest star to promote his rival's operation. Arnold was frustrated by this, but he also recognized that Weider was helping his career tremendously in other ways. Weider had set Arnold up in business and still used him extensively to endorse and promote many of the bodybuilding products he manufactured. Arnold also made personal appearances and gave seminars. After years of struggle, Arnold was now making a good living.

Arnold had enrolled in college, taking language, history, and business classes. When asked to write two essays for a class at UCLA on the person he most admired and the person he most hated, he wrote both essays on Weider.

That year, Arnold's brother Meinhard died in a car crash. A year later, his father died of a stroke. Gustav had come to London to see Arnold win a Mr. Universe title, but even after all his son's success, Gustav kept asking Arnold when he was going to get a real job. Arnold didn't go to the funeral of either family member, claiming that he couldn't break training. But Meinhard left a three-year old son, Patrick, and Arnold offered to support him. His mother accepted, and Arnold financed Patrick's high school and college education and later paid for him to move to California.

In 1973, Arnold was cast in his second movie. This time, he had a bit part in Robert Altman's hit

*When Arnold's brother Meinhard died, Arnold took
on the responsibility of supporting his nephew
Patrick (far right) into adulthood.*

movie *The Long Goodbye.* He played a goon who
terrorized private eye Philip Marlowe (portrayed
by Elliott Gould), and did quite well in a non-
speaking role. He also made an appearance as an
available bachelor on the television program "The
Dating Game."

Bodybuilding was becoming more popular,
and the biggest reason why was Arnold
Schwarzenegger. He loved to do publicity for his
sport and took every chance to appear before the
press. Arnold's charisma attracted the media, and

his arguments for his sport made viewers take bodybuilding more seriously.

Lucille Ball saw Arnold on a talk show and asked him to appear on a television special. She arranged for him to have a week of acting lessons and coached and directed him herself for the special. Arnold believes Lucy's interest in him was pivotal in his career.

Arnold also took intensive lessons before making the movie *Stay Hungry*. Luckily, his role called for him to play an Austrian bodybuilder, so the script did not have to account for his huge body and foreign accent. Still, he had to be credible in love scenes with the petite actress Sally Field and not look as if he was about to crush her instead of kiss her. (Later, Arnold would admit that romance on screen was not his forte. "I have a love interest in every one of my films—a gun.") In addition, Arnold had to play the violin. Two months of concentrated lessons allowed him to look as if he knew what he was doing.

**"I have a love interest in every one of my films—a gun."**

Arnold and the movie generally received good reviews. *Newsweek* said he was "surprisingly good as the muscle man with heart—and pectorals—of gold." Arnold won a Golden Globe Award for the most promising newcomer of the year—the only

*Arnold starred with Sally Field in the
feature film* Stay Hungry.

major acting award he has ever won. But still, no one in Hollywood was thinking about Arnold as a potential star. Indeed, two agents refused to take him on as a client, saying he would never make it.

## PUMPING IRON

In his next movie, Arnold played a role that he knew well. *Pumping Iron* was based on a book about bodybuilding by Charles Gaines, but the documentary was clearly meant as a showcase for Arnold to introduce the viewers to the world of bodybuilding and to show off his glorious self. George Butler produced and directed. The documentary had no script—it required only that the main participants simply be themselves. Nevertheless, Arnold continued taking acting lessons to prepare.

During the movie, the viewer sees Arnold train, tell jokes, study himself in the mirror, give a charity performance at a federal prison, and help aspiring bodybuilders learn their trade. The movie takes time out so Franco Colombu can perform a favorite trick: blowing up a hot water bottle until it bursts. The film culminates with the 1975 Mr. Olympia contest, which was held in Pretoria, South Africa.

Arnold was magnificent, free and easy in front of the camera. He showed off his magnetism

*In January 1977, Arnold accepts the Golden Globe
award as most promising newcomer for his role
in* Stay Hungry.

in every scene, whether pumping enormous weights or telling how he had wanted to come to the United States since the age of ten. In the competition, Schwarzenegger blew away his main rivals: Serge Nubret and Lou Ferrigno (who would himself later become an actor, starring in the television show "The Incredible Hulk"). Reg Park presented Arnold with the trophy, who then, to the surprise of all, announced that he was retiring from bodybuilding.

*In the film* Pumping Iron, *Arnold and Franco Colombu learn ballet moves from a dance instructor.*

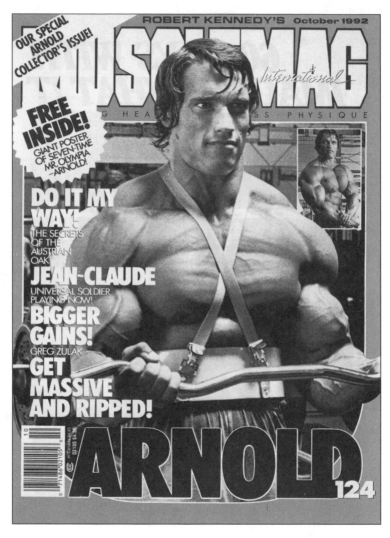

*The film* Pumping Iron *made bodybuilding very popular, but Arnold chose to leave the sport behind to become a Hollywood action hero.*

He was twenty-eight years old, had won every meaningful title several times over, and had no more mountains to climb in the bodybuilding world. *Pumping Iron* would make bodybuilding even more popular, but the sport would have to go on without its biggest star.

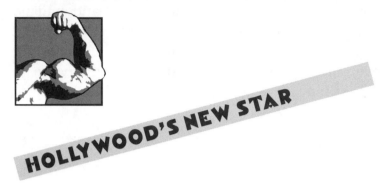

# CHAPTER FOUR

# HOLLYWOOD'S NEW STAR

A new type of action hero was on the rise in Hollywood. The same year Arnold broke through as an actor, he was eclipsed by the appearance of Sylvester Stallone as the boxer Rocky. Clint Eastwood was making an impact in spaghetti westerns (American westerns shot in Italy). Soon to follow was kung-fu fighter Chuck Norris. None of these men were particularly gifted at humor or romance, as their predecessors Sean Connery and James Coburn had been. But when these new stars beat the bad guys, they seemed to do it with a greater conviction.

Who would have thought Arnold could be a movie star? With his amazing body, he didn't look entirely normal. His strong accent made him sound as if he wasn't from the United States either. Most strong male actors with accents either had short careers or had been typecast as foreigners; they often landed the parts of the villains but never got to play the lead.

And while many other world-class athletes had gone on to attempt a career in films, few had met with any marked success. The long list of those who tried to become Hollywood action stars includes Jim Brown, Joe Namath, and Fred Williamson from football; Kurt Thomas from gymnastics; and Hulk Hogan from wrestling. Plus, there had never been a former bodybuilder who became an A-list star. Swimmers Johnny Weissmuller and Buster Crabbe made numerous Tarzan films, but like the flicks of Steve Reeves and Reg Park, they are B movies (low-budget films) . . . or worse.

*Pumping Iron* turned out to be a surprise hit when it opened. *New York* magazine said Arnold "lights up the film like neon every time he comes on-screen. . . . His physical power is balanced by great humor, prodigious charm, that same mixture of sweetness and sass, mock arrogance and mock innocence, that [Muhammad] Ali once possessed."

Arnold promoted the movie relentlessly, promoting his career at the same time. He wowed the press, winning over an initially unimpressed Barbara Walters, and letting Liz Smith feel his arm. "It was one of my proudest moments in journalism," she wrote. He made an appearance as a murder suspect (and European bodybuilder) on an episode of TV's "The Streets of San Francisco."

With the help of Douglas Kent Hall, he also wrote an autobiography, *Arnold: Education of a Bodybuilder.* Doubleday, his first publisher, rejected the manuscript when it came in. But Simon & Schuster accepted it, and Arnold convinced his publisher to send him to twenty-seven cities to publicize the book, not just the seven they initially planned. The promotion helped launch the book onto the best-seller list. Arnold boasted he could autograph four hundred copies an hour. "I just do 'Arnold' and then 'S' and a line and two 'g's," he said. He later went on to pen three other best-selling books.

Arnold's success allowed him to turn down some offers. He spurned Mae West, who was making her last and worst movie, *Sextette,* and rejected the lead in the TV series "The Incredible Hulk," claiming that the Hulk was supposed to be ugly and "I'm much too pretty." Arnold, however, failed to win the role of Superman, which went to Christopher Reeve. At the premiere of the movie, Arnold joked, "They did a good job of telling my life story."

**"I'm much too pretty."**

Arnold's next movie was a mistake for everyone involved. *The Villain* was supposed to be a spoof, but it is painfully unfunny. Arnold played the role of Handsome Stranger, who had to keep rescuing the beautiful Charming Jones (Ann-

*Arnold's role in the TV movie* The Jayne Mansfield Story *was perfect for him. He played a Hungarian bodybuilder opposite Loni Anderson.*

Margret) from a demented Cactus Jack (Kirk Douglas). Arnold looked embarrassed as an innocent cowboy, and the movie made no attempt to explain his decidedly un-Western accent. One critic said Arnold's horse outacted him and had more facial expressions. After Arnold became a superstar, he resurrected the hurtful review and pinned it on his office wall.

Arnold appeared briefly in the movie *Scavenger Hunt,* another eminently forgettable picture. His next project, though, seemed tailor-made for him. He played Mickey Hargitay in the TV movie *The Jayne Mansfield Story.* Hargitay, Mansfield's husband, was a Hungarian bodybuilder. Actually, Arnold had more in common with Mansfield (played by Loni Anderson), who combined a strong intelligence with a blinding ambition and a drop-dead physical presence. Arnold did well, making Hargitay seem like a three-dimensional character, although the movie probably would have been better had he not also provided the voice-over.

Arnold accepted the lead in *Conan the Barbarian,* expecting filming to begin in January 1981. Suddenly Universal Studios decided to move that date up by six months in order to tie promotion of the film in with the release of *Flash Gordon.* "All of a sudden, I had no time at all. I had to get big, and fast," thought Arnold. Arnold had been up for the role of Flash but lost his chance when he asked the diminutive producer Dino De Laurentiis why he needed such a large desk. Luckily, De Laurentiis didn't hold a grudge, as he was also the producer for *Conan*.

Arnold was thrilled to get the role. "I've never been wrong yet with my instincts, and they tell me this is going to be a really big film, a whole new phenomenon."

## COMEBACK

In order to get big fast, Arnold decided to make a comeback as a competitive bodybuilder. He decided to enter the 1980 Mr. Olympia contest, five years after having retired—but he also decided not to warn the other athletes.

Arnold showed up in Sydney, Australia, pretending he was covering the competition as a television commentator. A day before the contest started, Arnold admitted his unretirement to Reg Park, who was acting as a judge, master of ceremonies, and noncompeting guest poser. Park said, "Look, you've put me on the spot, Arnold, because everybody knows we're buddies. But I'm going to judge it the way I see it."

The other contestants protested Arnold's late entry. But they also felt he had little chance of winning. Boyer Coe, a rival, said, "He was not

*Arnold strikes an impressive pose at the 1980 Mr. Olympia competition. It was the last competition he entered, and he won.*

anywhere near to his former competition shape; we sort of felt sorry for him." Arnold had hurt his shoulder while training and took a cortisone shot which made him retain water. His legs, too, were stiff and swollen.

The favorite was Mike Mentzer, and Arnold quickly tried to psych Mentzer out. Offstage, Arnold teased him, saying, "With your belly, I think you'll be giving birth next week. What are you doing here?" Arnold also tricked defending champion Frank Zane. While the two posed together, Arnold told a joke that caused Zane to lose his composure and burst out laughing.

But Arnold was clearly rusty, too. He started to pose in a dark section of the stage, and Franco Colombu shouted at him to move. Arnold didn't hear him, so Colombu felt he had to rush out and tell him what to do. The audience stirred restlessly as Arnold held up Colombu's arm as if in triumph, let Colombu exit, and then moved to the better-lit part of the platform.

For the seventh time in his career, Arnold Schwarzenegger was named Mr. Olympia. This time, the unhappy audience booed and shouted "rigged." Boyer Coe bitterly spoke on the behalf of many other competitors when he said, "A fair placing for Arnold in that competition would have been eighth or ninth."

But many others agreed with the award. "I don't think Mentzer was in the same league, quite frankly," said Park. "There's a certain amount of 'presence' on stage which counts . . . and I don't think Mentzer had that appeal to the public. Arnold had that appeal even five years after retiring. He wasn't the Arnold of '75, but to my mind he was good enough to win."

George Butler, who had made *Pumping Iron,* captured Arnold's performance in the documentary *Comeback.* Arnold then returned to the United States to make *Conan the Barbarian,* the film that would finally make him a star.

## CONAN

*Conan* was based on stories written by Robert E. Howard, an amateur bodybuilder, in the 1930s. In the 1960s, they were turned into comic books. In the screenplay (written by Oliver Stone and director John Milius), Thulsa Doom (James Earl Jones) kills Conan's parents and forces the young boy to work on the "Wheel of Pain." The physical labor makes him strong, and he then undergoes training as a gladiator. When he wins his freedom, he sets off with a thief, a wizard, and a woman warrior (Sandahl Bergman) in order to steal a precious jewel. King Osric (Max Von Sydow) asks Conan to rescue his daughter from

*Arnold posed for this publicity shot for* Conan
the Destroyer. *The first Conan movie,* Conan the
Barbarian, *had made him a Hollywood star.*

Thulsa Doom. After many violent battles, Conan succeeds in all his tasks and cuts off the head of Thulsa Doom. Along the way, a stone-faced Conan expresses what he feels is best in life: "To crush your enemies, see them driven before you, and hear the lamentation of their women."

> **"To crush your enemies, see them driven before you, and hear the lamentation of their women."**
> **—Conan**

Arnold grunted more than he spoke, but then few characters had a lot of lines in this prehistoric, action-driven movie. Arnold performed his own stunts—jumping from a 40-foot- (12-m-) high tower, wrestling with huge snakes, getting kicked by a camel, thrown over by an elephant, and wielding a mean broadsword. On his first day of shooting, he was attacked by wolves, fell off a pile of rocks, and got a nasty cut that required stitches. The movie's opening line, "That which does not kill us makes us stronger" (a quote from the philosopher Friedrich Nietzsche) applied equally well to Arnold as it did to Conan.

This was Arnold's first starring role in a big-budget movie. The reviews of the $19-million film were not great, but the audience response was tremendous. A hit in the United States and overseas, it ended up grossing more than $100 million.

It even spawned a sequel, which teamed Arnold with Grace Jones and basketball legend Wilt Chamberlain. *Conan the Destroyer* was just as violent as the first film and no more intelligent. It, too, made more than $100 million.

# CHAPTER FIVE

SETTLING DOWN AND MOVING UP

On August 28, 1977, Arnold was invited to a celebrity event, the Robert F. Kennedy tennis tournament in Forest Hills, New York. There, he was introduced to an aspiring reporter, Maria Shriver. Although she was eight years younger than he, the two hit it off immediately.

Maria came from a distinguished family. She was the niece of the late president John F. Kennedy. Her father, Sargent Shriver, had created the Peace Corps during the Kennedy Administration and had run for vice president on the George McGovern ticket in 1972.

Arnold was smitten not only with Maria, but with her whole family. "They think so much about serving the public, about social work and being involved in politics and charitable activities. So much of their dialogue at home deals with 'What can we do for others?' and eventually this has an effect on you.

*Maria Shriver was active in politics, shown here soliciting support for her uncle Senator Edward Kennedy's presidential campaign in 1980.*

"Sports are a very selfish activity because you think only about yourself," he continued. "Even in team sports you are trying to make that score, and thinking about yourself as an athlete. You have to. In acting, it is even more exaggerated. So it was ideal for me to be exposed to that other side where no one talks about 'me,' they talk about 'you.'" Arnold volunteered to help with the Special Olympics, a cause dear to the heart of Maria's father. He was named honorary weight-lifting coach, later held benefits for the event, and appeared on the 1988 Special Olympics Christmas television special.

Maria got a job working for television stations, first in Philadelphia and then in Baltimore. She saw Arnold whenever he was on the east coast, and in 1978, they went on a ski trip to Europe. He also took her to the 1979 Cannes Film Festival in France, where crowds and the media adored his public appearances. Later that year, he received his college degree from the University of Wisconsin in Superior.

Perhaps the strangest thing about the attraction between the two—other than the great disparity in size between the man-mountain Arnold and the petite Maria—was that Arnold's politics were decidedly conservative Republican while members of Maria's family were famously liberal Democrats. He once joked, "Maria is well-rounded and gorgeous. I tell her that if we marry and have kids, with her body and my mind they'll have some real winners in the family."

Maria's father warned her that she should check whether he would be a good husband. "Dad said to pay attention to how Arnold treats the dog because that way I'll know how he'll treat the children," she said. Sargent Shriver gave the couple a labrador puppy, whom Arnold named Conan.

In 1981, Maria moved to the west coast to be nearer Arnold. She learned everything she could about Arnold's sport. In turn, "She reads my scripts," said Arnold, "and her opinion weighs heavily on all my decisions." Arnold also helped her lose weight to improve her appearance and take acting lessons. She got a job as a national correspondent for "PM Magazine" and then for "CBS Morning News."

On September 16, 1983, Arnold became a U.S. citizen. He kept his Austrian citizenship too,

*Arnold became a U.S. citizen in 1983.*

thanks to the help of his old friend Alfred Gerstl, now a powerful politician in Graz.

In December, Arnold lost control of the Jeep he was driving, and it rolled down a 40-foot (12 m) embankment. Luckily, Maria was only slightly hurt and Arnold just shaken up. A police officer who arrived on the scene didn't care much about the wreckage. He recognized Arnold and asked advice on how to improve his triceps.

## THE TERMINATOR

Arnold's next movie was also a breakthrough for him. In *The Terminator*, for the first time in his career, he played a villain (it would be his only villainous role until he played Mr. Freeze in the 1997 movie *Batman and Robin*); also, for the first time, he had a leading role in which he kept his clothes on.

Arnold played a cyborg, a humanoid robot, sent back in time to kill a woman (played by Linda Hamilton) whose unborn son was destined to become a hero. Arnold was extremely convincing as a scary killing machine who would stop at nothing to complete his mission. His fourteen words in the entire film included the famous warning, "I'll be back."

**"I'll be back."**
**—The Terminator**

*Arnold starred as an unstoppable cyborg in the science-fiction thriller,* The Terminator.

(In the movie he came back almost immediately, driving a Jeep through the glass doors of a police station.)

The director, James Cameron, wanted a movie about "the dark side of Superman." Originally, he wanted former football star O. J. Simpson to play the role, but Arnold was already such a star that his participation allowed the budget to be increased from $4 million to $6 million.

To prepare for the movie, Arnold spent three months training with all sorts of weapons. He not only wanted to know how to use them, but how to get used to them. "When you are reloading a gun, do not look at the gun," he explained. "Look at the victim. Practice a hundred times so you can reload without looking. Every gesture has to separate you from the rest of the bunch if you want to play a stud."

*The Terminator* was a huge hit. *Time* magazine called it one of the ten best flicks of the year, and Arnold was voted International Star of 1984 by the National Association of Theatre Owners.

## MORE FILMS

Arnold's next movie was a step back. In *Red Sonja,* yet another spin-off of *Conan*, he played the love interest while Brigitte Nielsen played the lead gladiator. Nielsen, a strong-willed twenty-one-year-old Danish model turned actress, was making her big screen debut in the role. Arnold was such a star that when he agreed to be in the movie, its budget was again increased to $6 million.

Maria asked Arnold not to make the movie, but Arnold was under contract to De Laurentiis. He flew to Rome, and soon he and Brigitte were involved in an affair. They went skiing in Austria after filming was wrapped, although Arnold then returned to the United States alone. He started shooting *Commando,* in which he took his killing powers, for the first time, to contemporary times. *Commando* was Arnold's most violent film by far, as one hundred characters bite the dust during the eighty-eight minutes of playing time. That's four times the death rate as in the Conan movies. In addition, as film critic Joe Bob Briggs pointed out, knives were "thrown into seventeen different body parts."

Arnold also tells many unfunny jokes about death in the movie. In one scene that was cut, he hacks off a man's arm, then beats the man with the arm in order to shut him up. The studio thought it was sick. Arnold thought it would be fun.

When the movie was released, Arnold tried to create a rivalry with Sylvester Stallone. Stallone had just come out with a violent action movie titled *Rambo: First Blood, Part II.* In an interview,

Arnold derided Stallone for using doubles and said *Commando* was a much better movie.

When Brigitte came to the United States to promote the opening of *Red Sonja*, she wanted to rekindle the romance with Arnold. Instead, Arnold concocted a way for her to meet Stallone, and the two quickly hit it off. Stallone rewrote the script for *Rocky IV* to include a part for her.

Arnold regretted the affair with Brigitte. He had been dating Maria for eight years and knew that his indiscretion had hurt her. On his thirty-eighth birthday, he flew Maria to Thal, Austria, and proposed to her while on a rowboat on the Thalersee, the local lake. They set a wedding date for more than nine months later, on April 26, 1986. Shortly after, Brigitte announced she was going to marry Stallone. (The marriage did not last long.)

Maria got two big breaks in a row. Within a month of becoming engaged, she won the job of co-anchor on the "CBS Morning News." She moved to New York where she had to get up at 3:00 A.M. in order to be on air at 7:00 A.M. On Fridays, she flew to Los Angeles to spend the weekend with Arnold. Arnold bought a $5 million mansion in Pacific Palisades as their new home. The seven-bedroom house had a swimming pool, tennis court, gym, and a two-acre garden complete with a beautiful stream. Among Arnold's neighbors were Stallone and Nielsen.

## WEDDING BELLS

The wedding was the big Hollywood event of the year, even though it took place at the Kennedy summer home in Hyannisport, Massachusetts. All the Kennedys were there, plus newspeople Tom Brokaw and Forrest Sawyer, columnist Abigail Van Buren, artist Andy Warhol, and actors Susan Saint James and Grace Jones. Arnold's best man was Franco Colombu. Oprah Winfrey read Elizabeth Barrett Browning's sonnet, "How Do I Love Thee?"

The one unpleasant note in the day was the absence of a friend of Arnold's, Kurt Waldheim. Waldheim had been secretary general at the United Nations for many years. After retiring, he returned to Austria, where he ran for president. Suddenly it was revealed out that throughout the past forty years, Waldheim had lied about his activities during World War II. He had been a Nazi storm trooper in a unit that carried out massacres in Yugoslavia. He had been wanted for murder and suspected of war crimes. When the news came out, the United States banned Waldheim from returning to the country, just two days before Arnold's wedding. Waldheim sent a present anyway, which was displayed at the reception: a statue of the couple dressed in traditional Austrian peasant clothing, Arnold in lederhosen and Maria in a dirndl.

*On April 26, 1986, Arnold Schwarzenegger and Maria Shriver pose for photographers after their wedding.*

Arnold praised Waldheim at the reception, which made several guests squirm in their seats. Afterwards, the couple flew to the Caribbean island of Antigua for their honeymoon.

## ARNOLD GOES HOLLYWOOD

Arnold's film career was now in high gear. In *Raw Deal,* he played a former FBI agent who returns to action in order to destroy a mob family. Although it was just another violent film, it gave Arnold a chance to wear a different sort of costume. "My wardrobe in *Conan* cost four dollars," Arnold joked, "while for *Raw Deal* I got twenty expensive suits made in Beverly Hills."

In 1987, Hollywood honored Arnold by giving him a star on the Walk of Fame on Hollywood Boulevard. *Predator* opened to huge box office business, and Arnold was already at work on *The Running Man.* In *Predator,* Arnold is a commando who has to take on an armor-clad reptilian bio-mechanoid, which has come from another planet and has wiped out a whole battalion of soldiers. Nearly fifty characters die in the film, which makes it one of Arnold's most gory, but his character is not directly responsible for all of the deaths.

*The Running Man* was also a violent, nasty movie. Based on a Stephen King novella, the futuristic film depicts a United States ruled by a

*In June 1987, Arnold was honored
with a star on the Hollywood Walk of Fame.*

fascist government. Arnold plays a prisoner who is hunted down on a sick television program. Featuring death by chainsaws and a stick of dynamite in the groin, the film was a flop at the box office, barely pulling in $40 million.

This same year, Maria lost her job at CBS, but she quickly got a new position as co-host of NBC's "Sunday Today." Her new network then added to her duties, asking her to anchor the nightly news on Saturday and also co-host the program "Yesterday, Today & Tomorrow." Maria was making close to half a million dollars a year, but that was still nowhere near the earning power of her husband. Arnold made about $6 million in 1988 and $35 million in 1989, according to *Forbes* magazine.

In *Red Heat,* for the first time, Arnold was paired with a comic actor, Jim Belushi, as his lead. Arnold played a Russian policeman sent to the United States to bring the killer of a fellow policeman to justice. Interestingly, Arnold made the most of his humorous lines, while Belushi's attempts at being funny fell flat.

*Red Heat* was filmed at the time of *glasnost,* as the Soviet government was offering more freedom to its citizens and offering to cooperate more with Western nations. The timing could not have been better for the film. *Red Heat* was the first western movie that was allowed to shoot in

*Arnold played a tough Russian policeman with the comic actor Jim Belushi in* Red Heat.

Moscow's famed Red Square, and on the first day of filming, Mikhail Gorbachev, the Soviet prime minister, announced the Russians were pulling out of Afghanistan. Arnold was paid $10 million for the film.

As a sign of Arnold's arrival as a superstar, the Friars Club in Hollywood gave him a roast. Comedians Henny Youngman, George Carlin, and Sid Caesar, along with co-stars Bruce Williams, James Earl Jones, and Danny de Vito, plus body-builders Jesse Ventura and Franco Colombu, took turns making jokes about Arnold. Milton Berle, Arnold's neighbor, emceed. Arnold took it all in stride, commenting "It's one of the rare nights when people can insult me and know that I won't kick their butts."

**"It's one of the rare nights when people can insult me and know that I won't kick their butts."**

Few other action heroes had ever attempted to make the switch to comedy: Clint Eastwood, Charles Bronson, Chuck Norris, and Steven Segal never tried. The only ones who laughed when Sylvester Stallone tried his hand at comedy in *Rhinestone* and *Oscar* were the critics. Audiences had the right not to expect much of Arnold in a comedy, but he surprised everyone with his per-formance in *Twins*. Ivan Reitman had directed

*Arnold and Danny DeVito were humorously cast as twin brothers in the comedy* Twins. *In this film, Arnold demonstrated his range as an actor.*

such hits as *Ghostbusters* and *Stripes*—both of which featured comic stars of "Saturday Night Live" and "Second City Television." He commissioned a script in which Arnold, a scientifically created genius, discovers he has an identical twin—played by the short, roly-poly Danny DeVito. The sight of the immense, friendly Arnold and the minuscule, scheming DeVito was funny in itself. Arnold showed that he could also be funny without being mean. He expressed real emotions, causing David Ansen of *Newsweek* to comment, "For the first time since *Stay Hungry* he's recognizable as a member of our species."

Arnold would continue to be typecast in movies, but now he could be typecast as either an action hero or an oversize comic actor.

# CHAPTER SIX

# THE GOOD LIFE

Besides making a lot of money from the movies, Arnold had always been a good businessman. As a bodybuilder, he headed a construction company. He promoted bodybuilding and bought the World Gym chain. Later, he invested in real estate. "Ninety percent of my investments have been very, very profitable," he admitted.

Arnold also knew how to spend the money he made. He bought fancy cars, including a Porsche and a Cadillac, and a Harley-Davidson motorcycle. One of his main indulgences is cigars. He often smokes two $25 cigars a day. He also gives money to charity, including the Simon Wiesenthal Center and the Hollenbeck Youth Center in East Los Angeles.

In the 1988 presidential election, Arnold Schwarzenegger helped campaign for George Bush. He made speeches in several states includ-

*Arnold joins a group of young people who have just been awarded the National Fitness Award. As chairman of the President's Council on Physical Fitness and Sports, Arnold visited all fifty states at his own expense to spread the message.*

ing Ohio, which he had been visiting for more than ten years to attend the Mr. Pro World contest. Some Republicans even claimed that Arnold's visit helped Bush carry Ohio.

In 1990, President Bush rewarded Arnold by naming him chairman of the President's Council on Physical Fitness and Sports. In May, Arnold went to the south lawn of the White House to lead the country in exercises. The press quickly nicknamed him "Conan the Republican" and suggested that he was thinking about a political career himself. Arnold joked he didn't want to be like Clint Eastwood, who then was mayor of Santa Monica. "If I were going to run, I'd go after something major—like the governor of California," he said.

He must have given that some more thought, as he later said, "Why should I run for governor? [I'd rather] have schmoozing sessions with film journalists who are quite different from political journalists who are always on the attack."

Meantime, Arnold was busy with a new career: fatherhood. Maria gave birth to Katherine Eunice Schwarzenegger on December 13, 1989. He hadn't had a chance to be with Maria a lot during the pregnancy because he had been in Mexico filming *Total Recall*. But Arnold was with her in the hospital when she delivered. In 1990, Maria signed a new deal with NBC that allowed her to

*Arnold gives his daughter, Katherine, a ride.*

be based in Los Angeles. Her many years of commuting were finally over.

Based on a story by Philip Dick, *Total Recall* takes place on Mars. A convoluted plot centers on a memory chip that has been implanted in Arnold's head. In the climax, it turns out that his wife (Sharon Stone) is a spy out to destroy him. "Consider that a divorce," he says as he shoots her.

Arnold's next film was another comedy, *Kindergarten Cop*. It's considered his best comedy, and it's his least violent film—only one person dies. Arnold, a police officer, has to go undercover as a kindergarten teacher to catch a bad guy. Amusingly, Arnold finds dealing with a bunch of screaming five-year-olds a lot harder than putting down crime. When the kids' antics get to him, Arnold bends over and pleads for sympathy, claiming he has a headache. "It might be a tumor," offers one of the tykes.

"It's not a tumor!" howls a shocked Arnold as the kids laugh hysterically.

Although Arnold doesn't watch a lot of television, he started showing up there more often. Kevin Nealon and Dana Carvey of "Saturday Night Live" created sketch characters that were largely based on Schwarzenegger. The medium-sized Nealon and smallish Carvey dressed in heavily padded sweatshirts and sweatpants and promised "to pump you up," all the while speaking

*In* Kindergarten Cop, *Arnold evacuates two of his students during a hilarious fire-drill scene.*

in a heavy Austrian accent. Arnold also took rib-
bing from David Letterman on Letterman's nightly show. He twice was the subject of Letterman's
famous "Top Ten" lists, including "Arnold
Schwarzenegger's Top Ten Rejected Movie Lines."
(Examples: "Can you please open this jar of olives
for me," and "Do you have any of those 'ouch-less'
Band-Aids?")

## *T2*

In 1991, Arnold and Maria had a second child,
Christina Aurelia. On July 4 that year, *Terminator 2* opened, and half of all the people who saw a
movie that weekend saw *T2*. The film had cost
$100 million to produce—making it the most
expensive film ever—but it turned out to be worth
that price. Many critics and fans consider *T2*
Arnold's best movie.

Arnold repeats his role as a killing machine of
the future. But this time, he is the good guy, sent
back in time to protect John Connor (played by
Edward Furlong) and his mother (Linda Hamilton) from an even more technologically developed
cyborg. This cyborg (Robert Patrick) can imitate
voices, walk through walls, and even reshape the
metal he's made from to stab people. He's also
impervious to pain and can piece himself together
after being blasted to bits.

The film makes a point that violence is bad—but it is the most violent film ever created to do so. "You just can't go around killing people," says John Connor. Arnold's Terminator doesn't understand. "Why?" he asks. Later, the boy informs the Terminator that he needs to speak with more style. Arnold learns to say "Hasta la vista, baby," which he does at the appropriate time—after finally dispatching the other cyborg.

> **"Hasta la vista, baby."**
> **—The Terminator**

One of the spin-offs from *T2* was a ride at Universal Studios in Orlando, Florida. Visitors are told "to survive, you must fight side by side with Arnold Schwarzenegger in a 3-D, 3-screen surround adventure that thrusts you beyond reality, beyond virtual reality and beyond imagination—into the middle of the greatest cyber-war of all time! You'll feel the blazing power of laser fire, dodge showers of plasma blasts from mini-Hunters. . . .The final explosive showdown will rock you senseless."

## BIG BUSINESS

In February 1992, Arnold opened a restaurant in Venice, California. Maria oversaw much of the design, while Arnold instructed that there be voices

*Arnold rides a motorcycle in this scene from* Terminator 2. *Many people feel that* T2 *is Arnold's best film.*

in the bathroom giving German lessons and hints on proper use of the facilities. Soon after, Arnold joined with Sylvester Stallone and Bruce Willis to create Planet Hollywood restaurants and franchise them around the world. In the New York Planet Hollywood, hamburger-eating guests can watch scenes from Arnold's movies on the dozens of television sets, while also seeing a cyborg costume from *T2* and James Dean's motorcycle from *Rebel Without a Cause.*

Arnold dabbled in other non-movie projects as well. He directed an episode for the television show "Tales from the Crypt," appearing briefly in the introduction. He also directed *Christmas in Connecticut,* a made-for-TV movie.

## ACTION HERO

Arnold wanted to build on the success of *T2,* but his next movie, *The Last Action Hero,* was the wrong vehicle. It attempted to be both funny and exciting but failed to be either. Arnold plays Jack Carter, a movie action hero, who along with a boy (Austin O'Brien), crashes cars and plays shoot-em-up—all without anyone getting hurt. This film too had an antiviolence theme, but the basic premise—that the boy finds a magic movie ticket that brings him on-screen—is reminiscent of Woody Allen's much more complex film *The Pur-*

*Arnold promotes his book,* Arnold's Fitness for Kids, *in a bookstore. An astute businessman, Arnold is involved in many enterprises, including the Planet Hollywood restaurant chain.*

*ple Rose of Cairo* (1985). The treatment of the premise is so unbelievable that people simply stayed away from *The Last Action Hero.*

This movie also cost nearly $100 million to produce, and advertising and promotion costs added close to another $50 million. The film bombed at the box office. Sony Pictures probably lost more than $100 million on the film, making it one of the largest flops of all time.

Another flop might have cost Arnold his standing in Hollywood, and several people were predicting that *True Lies,* his next movie, was headed for a bath. But the picture did a hearty $28 million on its opening weekend and fears for Arnold's career were allayed. In *True Lies,* Arnold somehow has convinced his wife (Jamie Lee Curtis) that he is a computer salesman. In the course of the film, we discover that he is a weapons expert, a trained pilot of top military aircraft, and a daredevil horseback rider as well as a spy for the United States's most secretive agency. His wife, a legal secretary, is aware of none of this. She gets involved with a used car salesman who is merely pretending to be a spy and invites her into his spy games.

As his character tracks down and destroys the bad guys, Schwarzenegger gets a chance to show off other talents. He speaks accentless Arabic and French—something he can't quite manage with English. He does a mean tango. Still, his wife is not happy when she learns that he has been a spy for the past seventeen years and never told her. He picks a poor time to inform her—after the bad guys seize them both and are about to torture and kill them—so she hauls off and slugs Arnold. Using all his acting technique, Schwarzenegger

*Arnold experienced the joys of fatherhood when he played a pregnant man in the comedy* Junior.

manages to convince the audience that she has actually hurt him although he outweighs her by about a hundred pounds.

In November 1993, Maria gave birth to a boy, Patrick. Feeling cramped, Arnold paid $3 million to buy the house next door, intending to use it largely as a guest house. He installed a basketball court in expectation of someday playing one-on-one with his son. The next year, he bought another adjoining house for $2 million.

Arnold had a cameo role in *Dave,* playing himself and advising against eating donuts. He had another comic role in *Junior,* playing a doctor who experiments upon himself and becomes pregnant. *Eraser* was a thriller in which Arnold plays a member of the witness relocation program who helps people who are going to give evidence in court against gangsters.

In June 1996, Arnold resigned his position as head of the President's Council on Physical Fitness and Sports. Bill Clinton, a Democrat, had replaced George Bush as president, and Schwarzenegger had other things to do.

In early 1997, Arnold now nearing age fifty, underwent surgery to repair a valve in his heart. He recovered quickly from the surgery. He needed to, because directors were waiting for him to star in four movies that he had already agreed to make and promote. Among the films to come: a remake

*Arnold, Maria, and their two daughters*

of *Planet of the Apes* and *Terminator 3. Batman and Robin,* in which Arnold played the villainous Mr. Freeze, was released in 1997 and became a summer hit.

When not engaged in the movie business, Arnold also looks over his investments, plays tennis with Maria, tends to his children, and enjoys the company of numerous good friends.

He still works out, usually pumping iron for

**"I'm having fun making movies that entertain people."**

*Autograph seekers hound Arnold as he arrives for the premiere of the action film* Eraser *(1996).*

*Arnold portrays the villain Mr. Freeze in*
Batman and Robin *(1997).*

an hour before breakfast every morning. Besides being one of the most successful movie stars of all time, Arnold is one of the richest people in the world today. Yet he is usually low-key about his success. "I'm not a very serious person," he says. "I'm having fun making movies that entertain people."

At age seventeen, Arnold planned a grand future for himself. Even at his most ambitious, however, he could not have dreamed of how successful he would become.

*Although he boldly predicted a fabulous future for himself when he was seventeen years old, Arnold Schwarzenegger is modest about his success.*

| | |
|---|---|
| 1947 | Arnold Alois Schwarzenegger is born in Graz, Austria, on July 30 |
| 1961 | Begins bodybuilding |
| 1964 | Enters first bodybuilding contest |
| 1965 | Serves in Austrian army; wins Junior Mr. Europe |
| 1966 | Moves to Munich, Germany, to train; wins Best Built Man of Europe, Mr. Europe, and International Powerlifting Championship |
| 1967 | Wins Mr. Universe (NABBA, amateur) |
| 1968 | Wins Mr. Universe (NABBA, professional), German Powerlifting Championship, and Mr. International; arrives in United States |
| 1969 | Wins Mr. Universe (IFBB, amateur) and Mr. Universe (NABBA, professional) |
| 1970 | Wins Mr. Universe (NABBA, profession- |

al), Mr. World, and Mr. Olympia; stars in *Hercules in New York*

1971 Wins Mr. Olympia

1972 Wins Mr. Olympia

1973 Wins Mr. Olympia; appears in *The Long Goodbye*

1974 Wins Mr. Olympia

1975 Wins Mr. Olympia

1976 Stars in *Stay Hungry,* for which he wins a Golden Globe Award for most promising newcomer of the year

1977 Stars in *Pumping Iron;* meets Maria Shriver

1979 Stars in *The Villain;* appears in *Scavenger Hunt*

1980 Wins his seventh and final Mr. Olympia; stars in *The Jayne Mansfield Story*

1982 Stars in *Conan the Barbarian*

1983 Stars in *Conan the Destroyer;* becomes U.S. citizen

1984 Stars in *The Terminator*

1985 Stars in *Commando;* stars in *Red Sonja;* writes *Arnold: The Education of a Bodybuilder*

1986 Stars in *Raw Deal;* marries Maria Shriver

1987 Stars in *Predator;* stars in *The Running Man;* receives his own star on Hollywood's Walk of Fame

| | |
|---|---|
| 1988 | Stars in *Red Heat;* stars in *Twins;* campaigns for Republican presidential candidate George Bush |
| 1990 | Stars in *Total Recall;* stars in *Kindergarten Cop;* named chairman of the President's Council on Physical Fitness and Sports |
| 1991 | Stars in *Terminator 2: Judgment Day* |
| 1992 | Directs *Christmas in Connecticut;* opens restaurant in Venice, California |
| 1993 | Stars in *The Last Action Hero;* appears in *The Last Party* |
| 1994 | Stars in *True Lies;* stars in *Junior* |
| 1996 | Stars in *Eraser;* stars in *Jingle All the Way* |
| 1997 | Has heart surgery; stars in *Batman and Robin* |

# A NOTE ON SOURCES

I used many materials in writing this biography. I started with Schwarzenegger's own book (co-authored by Douglas Kent Hall), *Arnold: The Education of a Bodybuilder* (New York: Simon & Schuster, 1977). I found additional information in the following biographies: Nigel Andrews's *True Myths: The Life and Times of Arnold Schwarzenegger* (Secaucus, NJ: Birch Lane, 1996); George Butler's *Arnold Schwarzenegger: A Portrait* (New York: Simon & Schuster, 1990); Craig A. Doherty and Katherine M. Doherty's *Arnold Schwarzenegger: Larger Than Life* (New York: Walker, 1993); and Wendy Leigh's *Arnold: An Unauthorized Biography* (Chicago: Congdon and Weed, 1990). For insight into Arnold's films, I consulted John L. Flynn's *The Films of Arnold Schwarzenegger* (New York: Citadel Press, 1996). The best introduction to Arnold as a bodybuilder is the movie *Pumping Iron* (1977).

# FOR MORE INFORMATION

## BOOKS

Andrews, Nigel. *True Myths: The Life and Times of Arnold Schwarzenegger.* Secaucus, NJ: Birch Lane, 1996.

Doherty, Craig A. and Katherine M. Doherty. *Arnold Schwarzenegger: Larger Than Life.* New York: Walker, 1993.

Flynn, John L. *The Films of Arnold Schwarzenegger.* New York: Citadel Press, 1996.

Schwarzenegger, Arnold, and Douglas Kent Hall. *Arnold: The Education of a Bodybuilder.* New York: Simon & Schuster, 1977.

## INTERNET RESOURCES

**Arnold Classic Website**
**http://www.schwarzenegger.com/**
This official Arnold Schwarzenegger site provides lots of information on Arnold and his movies, as well as his tips about bodybuilding and lists of up-coming events.

**The Arnold Page**
**http://www.geocities.com/Hollywood/6216/arnold.htm**
If you're an Arnold fan, you'll find everything you want to know about his movies, restaurants, and latest attractions at this site.

**Internet Movie Database**
**http://us.imdb.com/**
Visit the Internet Movie Database and search under Schwarzenegger for a list of his movies and a full description of each.

**T2-3D at Universal Studios Florida**
**http://www.usf.com/att/t2.html**
This site describes Universal Studio's latest attraction—a 3-D surround-screen movie that puts you in the middle of a T2 cyber-war.

# INDEX

**Page numbers in *italics* indicate illustrations.**

## ABOUT THE AUTHOR

Daniel Bial is an author, agent, and editor who has spent twenty years in publishing. He has written several books for children including biographies of Anfernee Hardaway and Grant Hill. A graduate of Trinity College, he lives in New York with his wife, Abby, and daughter, Miriam.

97029323